The Old House Book of
Bedrooms

The Old House Book of
Bedrooms

Lawrence Grow, General Editor
Ellen Beasley, Consultant

WARNER BOOKS

A Warner Communications Company

Designed by Carl Berkowitz

Warner Books, Inc.
75 Rockefeller Plaza
New York, N.Y. 10019

 A Warner Communications Company

Printed in the United States of America

First printing: October 1980

10 9 8 7 6 5 4 3 2 1

Library of Congress Cataloging in Publication Data

GROW, LAWRENCE.
  THE OLD HOUSE BOOK OF BEDROOMS.

    1. BEDROOMS.   2. INTERIOR DECORATION.
I. BEASLEY, ELLEN II. TITLE.
NK2117.B4G76   747.7'7   80-5746
ISBN 0-446-51216-8 (hardcover)
ISBN 0-446-97553-2 (pbk. U.S.A.)
ISBN 0-446-97780-2 (Canada)

Contents

Preface

Those who make old houses their homes frequently lament the lack of useful printed material concerning period interior design. At one extreme are technical treatises invaluable to individuals undertaking significant restoration projects; at the other extreme are informal articles often devoted more to the application of colorful cosmetic touches than to the essential matters of design. *The Old House Book* series, of which *Bedrooms* is the second volume, aims to provide the home decorator and restorer with fundamental information in an historical context. Information on how and in what manner families lived in the past — whether 75 or 250 years ago — is a prime requisite in such a volume. So, too, are examples of how the past is being interpreted today in homes throughout North America. *The Old House Book of Bedrooms* presents such a blend of background information and present-day experience.

In bringing together widely diverse materials, both historical and contemporary, the assistance of the Historic American Buildings Survey, Washington, D.C. (now part of the National Architectural and Engineering Record) has been invaluable. Al Chambers and Carter Christianson of the HABS staff, and Mary Ison of the Prints and Photographs Division of the Library of Congress have assisted in retrieving useful visual material. Equally enthusiastic and helpful have been those members of local, regional, and national historic preservation societies and consultants in the field who have tracked down fresh and imaginative approaches to period interior design across the country. This was often difficult as only houses which serve as private dwellings and which have not been widely publicized have been photographed and documented for this volume. For sharing their expertise, Gary Kray, Anne Baker, George Pearl, John Conron, and the Valenta family are especially thanked.

Introduction

The refinishing and furnishing of a room in an old house to reflect the style of an earlier time has been a favorite pastime of Americans since the late 1800s. Only in recent years has this activity, most often pursued on a do-it-yourself basis, become both commercialized and professionalized. An enormous array of reproduction materials of varying quality and authenticity is available to be used today, and expert advice—presented in the form of books and articles and offered by restoration consultants and interior designers—is to be had for the asking. It is no longer fashionable, however, to speak of "decorating" a room; if one cannot "preserve" a period interior, then the acceptable alternative is to "restore." The change in language represents a decided change in approach to the very serious and complicated problems of historical reconstruction. The new emphasis on period details also reflects a much greater public appreciation of valuation of past building styles and structures. This is all to the good if it leads one away from a cosmetic approach to historical re-creation, the surface application of a 20th-century reproduction finish to an older form. At the same time, however, there has to be an attempt made to steer away from the deadly dull and questionable effects sometimes produced by zealous antiquarians bent on recapturing a particular period of time. Houses that are homes are meant for living and must, if they are to be liveable, meet our needs for comfort and convenience.

How, then, does one approach this serious business? Even the experts will admit that the correct details for any particular are interpreted differently from time to time. Since the Centennial Exhibition of 1876, for instance, nearly each generation of decorators, amateur and professional alike, has seen the American Colonial style in a different manner. Today we laugh at the oriental-carpeted, Priscilla-flounced interiors of the 1920s through the '50s that called themselves "Colonial." Everyone knows today that the average colonist used only straw mats or an occasional rag rug on the floor and, if anything at all at the window, nothing more than a straight-hanging piece of homespun. But is what we are likely to do now going to be similarly scoffed at in the year 2000? Possibly. Even well-documented canvas floorcloths and painted fireboards, rediscovered in the 1970s, are beginning to look somewhat suspect and rather self-conscious in the 1980s. Were they really to be found in the average home during the 18th century? In the shifting fashion of period decoration, there is little that is sacred and much that is profane. Yet there remains one constant in any given

Above: East bedroom, Ruggles Mansion, Columbia Falls, Maine, 1818, built by Aaron Simmons Sherman. A secondary bedroom rather than the principal chamber, this room was always furnished more simply than that set aside for the owner of the house and his wife (see page 81). The interior has been redecorated several times.

Left: A late-18th-century canopy bed and lowboy with dressing glass.

project, one immovable object to be studied—the building itself. It is unlikely that a house is unique in every respect. It may have been modeled on another building which may or may not have been more stylistically perfect. Models of excellence existed in the past and fortunately survive today. Most of these dwellings reflect an economic and social level far above that achieved by most Americans in the past. They are limited, therefore, in usefulness for today's needs, but they contain helpful comparative evidence of what was. Every attempt has been made in these pages to include simpler vernacular structures which are less exceptional but more typical of the kinds of homes known in North America throughout 300 years of history. Studied together with the exemplars of architectural taste, also illustrated here, they yield striking evidence of the ways in which period interior design and building have evolved.

One of the verities of modern architectural practice is that form should follow function. In old house restoration, function should, in large degree, follow form. Novelist Edith Wharton didn't really care for much of anything Colonial or Victorian in America; her considerable taste was anchored in the classical aesthetic of the Italian Renaissance. In explaining matters of style, however, in *The Decoration of Houses,* a 1902 volume written with Oliver Codman, she brilliantly summarized her basic approach to design: "To conform to a style, then, is to accept those rules of proportion which the artistic experience of centuries has established as the best, while within those limits allowing free scope to the individual requirements which must inevitably modify every house or room adapted to the use and convenience of its occupants." The decoration or design of a period interior, Wharton argues, should follow architectural proportion as far as possible "in contradistinction to the modest view of house-decoration as superficial application of ornament."

Every period building—freestanding single family, attached, or one made up of multiple units—is likely to possess some overall period "look." The interior spaces of the average old house may not express those rules of proportion which Mrs. Wharton considered "best," but they, too, are likely to have been based on a particular style of the day, however roughly executed. Restoration purists may insist on removing all that they consider to be the excrescences of time, the structural modifications of several or many generations, but most people are content to make do with the given as long as this has some sort of stylistic coherence. Most of the changes made in an old-house interior over the years are likely to have been cosmetic rather than structural, and these can be altered at much less cost and time.

Each person approaching the restoration of a period house must seek a level of adaptation appropriate for that house or interior space and one which is economically feasible of accomplishment. Preservation of what is structurally original is critical; restoration to a historically valid state is also important, but may be a matter of degree. Old buildings can be made into remarkably functional dwellings without doing an injustice to their basic character. For instance, the fundamental form of a bedroom in a house of the early 19th-century Federal period, usually a very square space, is a given; so, too, are a fireplace with an Adam-style mantel, and fairly large sash windows with perhaps 6-over-6 lights. Other elements in the room's make-up may be less fixed in time. The fireplace may

Above: Guest bedroom, "Riverdale" (Allison Mansion), Indianapolis, Indiana, 1911-14, H. L. Bass, architect, photograph dates from c. 1916. In the early 20th century there was a return to the elegant formality of the Georgian Colonial period. This is one of five bedrooms situated on the second story of a Colonial Revival mansion. Everything possible was done to make the room as inviting and distinguished as possible — from parquet flooring to the use of a European canopy bed with side hangings. As in Colonial-period rooms, the furnishings are arranged in relation to the fireplace.

Left: Field bed and tester, bedside stand, and dressing table with dressing glass, early 19th century.

or may not be fitted with a stove; there is a wide range of appropriate period paint colors to choose from as well as reproduction papers of varying complexity for the walls; a four-poster canopied bed could be appropriately used, but so might a low-poster or a draped field bed. Furnishings can represent the taste of several generations and certainly include objects which are deemed Colonial. Closets were by no means unknown at the time and, if absent from the room, can probably be worked into the space without doing an injustice to its proportions. Modern techniques now allow for the introduction of electric lighting without what Mrs. Wharton termed in 1902 the "harsh white glare."

There are historically-valid ways of treating every room in an old building of whatever period, and these are outlined in the following pages. As long as the proportions, the basic structural character of a house is respected, however, the refinishing and furnishing of interior spaces can be pursued with assurance and flexibility. Most of the interiors shown in these pages are of private homes used on an everyday basis. They demonstrate that the art of restoration is a subtle balancing act between the needs of the present and the dictates of the past.

Back bedroom, private residence, southeast Massachusetts, c. 1710-15, with additions c. 1725 and 1830, photograph dates from c. 1900. Although prettified to some degree for the photographer, this New England child's room remains Spartan in appearance, as were many such bedrooms for children during the 18th and 19th centuries. No attempt, for instance, had been made over the years to hide the framing or girt in the wall. Another view of this room is seen on page 45.

1.
The Bedroom: A History

The bedroom, the most personal of interior spaces to be found in any house, has often remained beyond the reach of the professional restorer or even the decorator. Usually found on the second floor of a period residence, it is sometimes the last of the rooms to be "fixed up," more public spaces on the first floor, historically known as the principal or living rooms, having been given priority since they are all that most visitors see. The time when a bedroom also served as a sitting room has long passed, although this is not to say that rooms for sleeping should not also be used for reading, sewing, and other quiet pursuits. Children "go to their rooms" for more than rest; why not adults? Martha Washington found her bedroom the only decent and quiet place in which to entertain guests to tea when spending a winter at her husband's Valley Forge headquarters. The General and his cohorts could stomp around the first floor with abandon.

Bedrooms in the earliest North American homes were practically nonexistent. Settlers intent on clearing land had little time to build homes with distinct and personal living areas. Sleeping quarters were most likely to be found in a corner of a one-room-deep dwelling, not far from the fireplace which supplied heat and a place for cooking. The whole family may have slept

Principal room, Thomas Clemence House (Clemence-Irons House), Johnston, Rhode Island, c. 1680. This was the only room in which the family originally lived. There is a half-story above, but the use of this space is not known; it might have been used as a dormitory for children. A lean-to was added at some later time.

together in a space not unlike that devoted solely to dining today. A traditional bed was a luxury in the 17th century and in later years as the frontier moved West. If a bed existed, it stood off to one side of the all-purpose living room/kitchen/dining room/bedroom and held more than one tired soul. The medieval sleeping alcove with hangings and bed clothing, related to the draped bed form of the Colonial period, was rarely found in the New World. The typical arrangement more closely resembled that amusingly portrayed in the 1934 film *It Happened One Night,* in which Claudette Colbert and Clark Gable resorted to the use of bed linen for temporary walls and privacy. If attic space was available, it might have been crammed full with children who slept there in dormitory fashion.

Varying provisions for distinct and separate sleeping areas were provided after the first years of settlement. Homes in Southern coastal areas were somewhat more advanced in this respect, at least those of prospering farmers. Planters early provided a first-floor sleeping "chamber," and some 18th-century tidewater homes in Maryland, Virginia, and the Carolinas still include such a room. It was cooler to sleep in at night than an upstairs room and, for the care of the elderly or sick, it was a convenience during the day.

In many areas of the deep South and the Southwest, houses one-story high were built during the years of original settlement. Primarily found in villages and the country, they could be added on to in a horizontal direction almost indefinitely. This is seen most clearly today in the New Mexican adobe hacienda where one room was often added to another in a straight line. By the late 18th century, a wing might have been extended to an earlier central

building at one or both sides to form an L- or U-shaped structure. Later, after the arrival of the Americans in the mid-19th century, a second story was sometimes added to at least part of the building. The majority of the adobe homes, however, remained low-lying and simple in plan. A better known example of the one-story dwelling is the late 19th-century bungalow, with bedrooms at the rear of the house far from the street or road. It is more commonly encountered today in both the urban and rural South than the two-story residence. Its popularity spread throughout the country in the 20th century, as did the later Western "ranch-style" house.

From almost the earliest days of settlement, city dwellers were considerably more advanced in their domestic arrangements than country people. Land was more expensive, and building almost immediately proceeded in a vertical rather than a horizontal direction. With the development of house plans along architecturally-consistent lines in the 18th century, the divisions between various domestic functions—sleeping, eating, reading, entertaining—became more distinct. Until at least the late 19th century, however, a bedroom, at least that for the master and his mistress, was intended to serve more than a nighttime purpose. This was especially true in rural and village homes which generally grew in size more slowly than those of the city and its suburbs. Central heating came first to the urban areas and freed the family from the necessity of living in limited space during at least the colder months.

With the building of new homes and the enlargement of the old in the East during the 18th century, provision for a "chamber floor" became customary. Within the family, the parents' room was the best. Here could be displayed the finest four-poster

Two-room house, Boundary County, Idaho, as photographed in 1939. On each new frontier to the West, most settlers started out on a small scale and built simple houses merely sufficient to shelter them.

First-floor bedroom, Juan Lopez House, Trampas, New Mexico, as photographed in 1943. In many areas of the South and West, a majority of homes were built with only one story, a room being added to another on the same level when necessary. This is especially true of early adobe buildings in the Southwest. Houses with relatively-low profiles are also commonly found in the area now known as the Sunbelt, where the bungalow became so popular in the early 20th century.

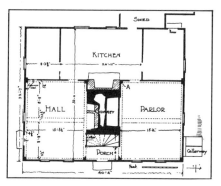

First-story plan, John Barnard House, Hartford, Connecticut, c. 1673, lean-to added c. 1767. Sleeping chambers in this early Colonial were provided over each of the two principal rooms, the one over the parlor being elaborately finished with pine paneling.

bed and its attendant hangings — valance, tester, head cloth, and curtains. This room might also contain a chest, cupboard with drawers, a looking glass, and several pieces of seating furniture. Recent research on furniture usage indicates that both the rocker and the upholstered wing chair, often fitted for use as a commode, were first used in such a bed-sitting room during the 18th century; each was regarded as an informal piece of furniture unsuitable for the principal first-floor rooms. Only later, in the first decades of the 19th century, did these forms move to the more formal parlor or sitting room.

It is clear that lavish attention was not devoted to the bedroom floor in the early years. Whereas a parlor in an early 18th-century Connecticut house might contain raised paneling, the walls in the room above it were likely to have been finished off with whitewash or, at best, 3-foot horizontal wainscoting. In furnishings, a child's

room might contain little more than a bedstead, a trundle, chest, and chair. Facilities for washing were, for all practical purposes nonexistent except on a temporary basis, a movable tub being provided for the occasional bath and a washstand holding the common pitcher and bowl. Closets for the storage of clothes were a rarity, a chest being first used for this purpose, and later, in the best bedrooms, a cupboard or linen press.

It is no wonder, then, that bedrooms were the focus of so much domestic improvement in the 19th century. The bedroom as a center of feminine domesticity had its roots in earlier times, but during the Victorian era, a period of almost frenetic housewifely activity, a gentler touch prevailed over the functional. A virtual cult of motherly love developed around what in the literature of the mid- to late-19th century became known as the "mother's room." *Beautiful Homes or Hints in House*

Section drawing, Smith-Painter House, West Haven, Connecticut, c. 1685. In contrast to the parlor, the space devoted to the bedrooms was merely functional and barely decorative. The lean-to, original to the house, includes a sleeping chamber.

Furnishings (1878), an exceptionally popular book by Henry T. Williams and Mrs. C. S. Jones, sang the praises of

that most delightful retreat, which as the heaven of rest for each afflicted or sorrowing member of the flock, is to be looked back upon and fondly remembered in the "after-time," when in recalling one by one the hallowed land-marks belonging to the old homestead, this spot stands out prominently above all the rest, as the sacred casket in which are enshrined the smiles and tears of childhood's hour, the joys and sorrows of youthful days, the confessions and confidences of maturer years, all poured into the fond mother's ear and hallowed by her admonitions and prayers.

No mention is made of how "mother" felt about it all, but presumably she found contentment of some sort in what became exceedingly fussy surroundings.

The four-poster, both the traditional type with hangings and the Federal canopied field bed without curtains, continued in popularity during the 19th century, particularly in rural areas of the Northeast and South. In the latter region, the bed might be provided with mosquito netting to shield the sleeper from marauding insects. Gradually the traditional four-poster was replaced in many homes by elaborately carved Rococo Revival and Renaissance Revival bedsteads in black walnut, rosewood, or grained imitations of the same woods. Such a monumental piece, often with a towering headboard, was usually accompanied by others in a "suite" (usually pronounced "suit") specially purchased for the room: a dressing bureau, wardrobe, washstand, nightstand, rocker, and loveseat or sofa. Marble tops on some of the pieces were as practical an addition as Formica is today on bathroom or kitchen counters.

"Suits" of varying quality and cost were first offered widely in the 1840s, and some, made of pine, were considered affordable by the average family. Varnish or painted pieces of this sort were known as "cottage" furniture and became a staple of 19th-cen-

"Design for a Bed" from George Hepplewhite's *The Cabinet-Maker & Upholsterer's Guide* (third edition, 1794). The festooned valance and the well-turned posts would have been admired by American colonists enamored of neoclassical taste in furnishings and decoration. Hepplewhite's designs were well known in America by the late 18th century. The use of hangings at the foot of the bed, as well as at the sides, however, was then falling into disfavor in the New World.

Master bedroom, private residence, south-eastern Massachusetts, c. 1710-15, photograph dates from c. 1900. A field bed with arched tester frame is typical of Federal-period taste in furnishings. Usually the frame is simply draped rather than being festooned. Nearly all the furnishings in the room date from the late 18th or early 19th century. In the late 1800s, this "look" was considered "Colonial"; for a view of how the room appears now, see page 44.

Bedroom/sitting room, the same Massachusetts home, photograph c. 1900. This room and others were added about 1725 when the house was enlarged from a simple two-room-deep dwelling with the chimney at the gable end to a Georgian Colonial with a center chimney. The sophisticated paneling of the room end is representative of that introduced to master bedrooms of affluent households during the 18th century. The room illustrated came to be used as a sitting room in the late 19th century.

Northwest bedroom, "Rattle and Snap," near Columbia, Tennessee, 1845. The popularity of the canopy bed survived the various changes of fashion during the Victorian period. In style this bed is similar to the design advanced by Hepplewhite, but without foot curtains and a valance in festoons. In decoration the room reflects more the lingering influence of the Colonial Revival than the Greek Revival period of the house itself.

Southeast green chamber, "Roseland" (The Bowen House), Woodstock, Connecticut, mid-19th century, Joseph C. Wells, architect. "Cottage furniture" of the type illustrated here was especially recommended by A. J. Downing in his influential *Architecture of Country Houses* (1850); both the sleigh bed with headboard and footboard of equal height and the dresser with mirror are part of a set painted red with line decoration in gold. Sets of this sort have rarely survived intact.

Bedroom, Governor Henry Lippitt House, Providence, Rhode Island, 1874-75. The set of furniture used in this bedroom today is a great deal simpler in form and finish than that used originally in most mansions of the period. The set closely resembles the Renaissance Revival pieces mass produced by late-19th-century furniture manufacturers. In other ways, however, the room was richly appointed — with carved wood cornices, heavy draperies, recessed shutters, a marble fireplace, chestnut and black-walnut moldings, and a painted ceiling.

tury manufacturers. So-called Grand Rapids furniture, named for the place in the Midwest where it was widely produced, was known and used throughout the country. Fashionable suites such as these were national in reputation and reflected little of the regional differences known earlier in handcrafted or shop-produced pieces.

From the 1860s on not only furniture but floors, windows, and doorways were candidates for fabric coverings of various sorts. Floors in children's rooms might have been covered only with a few scatter rugs—one at each side of the bed and a third before the hearth—but carpeting reigned supreme in the master bedroom. Here, too, a cast-iron stove or coal grate provided welcome heat in cold months. A primitive hot-air central heating system might have been in use by mid-century. Everything possible was done to make the room as cosy and comfortable as possible.

Wallpaper, much less costly after the introduction of steam-powered presses in the 1840s, could be applied to walls previously whitewashed. In this, as in other decorative impulses of the mid-19th century, the preference was for materials in the French style. Fabrics and papers employed strong reds, blues, greens, and golds in small patterns. The prosperous Victorian housewife could and did indulge her fancy for printed cottons, solid velvet and plush, finely worked wool and silk damasks. Such fabrics were used not only for window curtains, draperies, and portieres between connecting rooms, but also for pillows, throws, and upholstery. Only in the summer, when heavy draperies and carpets were removed, did lightness and light prevail. During this season, of course, wives were as likely to be working in the garden or kitchen as they were to be sewing or reading in the bedroom.

Servants were available to help the middle- or upper-class Victorian housewife dust and air the lavishly-decorated rooms. Only gradually, in the 1880s and '90s, was the use of heavy appointments questioned by the social arbiters. Charles L. Eastlake, the English furniture designer and architect widely followed in America, announced in 1878 that "A room intended for repose ought to contain nothing which can fatigue the eye by complexity." He was particularly vexed by "the practice of encircling toilet tables with a sort of muslin petticoat, generally stiffened by a crinoline of pink or blue calico." Other critics joined in the campaign for simplicity, notably Clarence Cook in his vastly popular *The House Beautiful* (1881). Cook noted that his good friend Charles McKim, the famous architect, had turned to the use of common pine for the furnishings of his new houses and was returning to a spare style not known since the early years of the century.

From the 1840s through the 1880s, mahogany, rosewood, and black walnut were the woods most favored for woodwork and furniture in the best rooms, including the master bedroom. Such elegant materials satisfied a popular desire for luxury in the European manner admired by all citizens of any social pretension. Home owners who could not afford the use of fine hardwoods turned instead to grained and/or varnished imitations of them in pine, cedar, or redwood. Oak, the cheapest of the hardwoods, gradually came into favor; stained a dark color, it resembled mahogany. Fashion, however, is fickle. When embraced by a large part of the public, it is no longer chic or desirable. This situation, combined with a yearning for a more patriotic American style born of the Centennial era, ushered in the Colonial Revival and Mission Revival fashions. By the 1890s the vogue for a simpler style was well established. This was as evident in the master bedroom as elsewhere in the late-Victorian residence. The wing chair, termed by Cook "sort of a half-way house between the bed just left, or just about to be entered, and the world of active work," returned to the boudoir. So, too, did Windsor chairs, the canopy bed, and scatter rugs. Unadulterated oak, pine, and redwood replaced finer woods; printed cottons were substituted for cretonne and damasks.

Structural changes were also undertaken in the late-Victorian bedroom. Closets were added or enlarged. After the turn of the century, indoor plumbing and bathrooms removed the need in many homes for washstands and, eventually, dressing tables or stands. The fireplace, however — whether fitted with a stove, a coal or gas grate, or even closed up with only the mantle intact — remained the central decorative element in most rooms. During the Colonial Revival, in fact, a fake Adamesque mantel was sometimes installed in rooms where the fireplace served no useful function.

Well into the 1930s fashions in bedroom furnishings continued along basically simple lines. Abhorrence of the mid-Victorian taste for overstuffed furniture and draped appointments led to the widespread use of metal beds and, in time, to blond "Hollywood"-style bedroom sets of either pseudo-Colonial or moderne design. These were considered not only more up-to-date but also as more healthful or sanitary. Concern

about disease — whether transmitted from feather mattresses or dust-laden draperies — seriously troubled the public. Warnings attached to pillows and mattresses concerning their sanitary contents were religiously safeguarded in place by several generations of children fearful of a visit from the police if these tags were ripped off. White or light pastels became the predominant paint color for both woodwork and walls, a color scheme which strengthened yet another image of the housewife — as sickroom nurse and hygienist.

The 20th century also witnessed improvements in sleeping accommodations for children. Except in the homes of the wealthy, these rooms were makeshift in furnishing and were not usually heated. A private room for each child eventually became accepted gospel, and, even in those homes where it was not possible to provide such amenities, these previously barren spaces were considerably spruced up. Special sets of commercial bedroom furniture for children had been available since the mid-19th century, but, in popular practice, a low-post bed, indistinguishable from that used by the hired man, had been provided. In the 1920s a child might have his own bed and dresser set as well as a matching desk and chair. By this point in time the bedroom — for both adults and children — had attained its maximum size and specialized use.

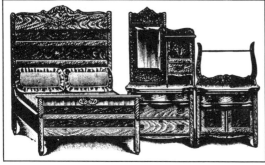

Bedroom suite as advertised by Sears, Roebuck & Co. in 1902. Besides the bed ($3.75) there was also a cheval dresser with a side cupboard ($8.35) and a commode or washstand without mirror ($3.40). The pieces were available in oak, stained golden or in imitation of mahogany. The applied decoration was machine-made, as was the furniture itself, and for the manufacturer to describe it as "elaborately carved" was to indulge in hyperbole of the highest order. Such a suite, nevertheless, was considered quite desirable by the average home owner and just as enthusiastically acquired.

Above (left): Toilet table from *Beautiful Homes* (1878) by Henry T. Williams and Mrs. C. S. Jones. The weight and complexity of such draping thoroughly oppressed the highbrow critics of the time.

Above: "A bed is the most delightful retreat known to man," an illustration from Clarence Cook's *The House Beautiful* (1881). The furnishings follow the simple lines advocated by Charles Eastlake in the 1860s and '70s. The semi-naturalistic design of the wallpaper and frieze is rigorously contained and defined by the picture molding and cornice.

Above (left): "A Half-way House," an illustration from *The House Beautiful.* The return of the Colonial-period wing chair and other "antique" furnishings to the bedroom was recommended by the tastemakers in the years following the Centennial Exhibition. *Center (left):* A piece of furniture which combined the functions of a wardrobe and a linen press was termed a hanging-press in Eastlake's *Hints on Household Taste.* The design is free of what he called "extravagant curves," "strips of paltry and meaningless scrollwork," and a "heavy and uninteresting cornice." *Below (left):* Advertisement for Farrell & Turnbull Plumbing, Duluth, Minnesota, 1903. The introduction of steam heating sometimes required the rearrangement of interior layouts; space had to be provided for radiators. Their design and ease of use were also important considerations for the home owner. The lady of the house found radiators much less of a fuss than stoves or open-hearth fires, but there was concern about leaking valves and spitting steam. Bedrooms were the last to be heated in the modern manner and, even when radiators were installed, they were often kept closed until the evening hours. *Above:* A typical bedroom of the late 19th century. Metal beds were lighter and easier to keep clean than most wood models. Lace curtains, hung straight from rings on rods without a valance or cornice, allowed for more light and air than heavy draperies.

2.
The Essentials: Windows, Doors, Ceilings, and Floors

Basic decisions on how to proceed with the restoration and furnishing of a period interior must begin on the most elementary level—a study of the structural character of the space. Although there may have been substantial remodeling over the years, it is likely that the essential core of a building has remained in place and that enough of its outlines can be read to serve as guidelines. The master bedroom may have changed more than some other areas, but the remaining rooms for sleeping are more than likely to have been benignly neglected.

The changes that have occurred will probbly not require extensive work unless one is determined to restore a room *in toto* to a narrow time period. Windows may have been enlarged or repositioned; the arrangement of space may have been altered for the addition of closets, a dressing room, or bathroom—and this means, in most cases, the use of dry walls and not bearing walls: ceilings may have been plastered over, lowered, or raised; doors may now appear where there were none 100 years ago; narrow oak flooring may have replaced random-width white or yellow pine boards. Any decision of just how much restoration needs to be done should be based on how fitting is any one of these "improvements." A bedroom built in a house of the Greek Revival style, for instance, should not have double-hung window sash with a single large pane but a minimum of four small ones. On the other hand, closets that have been made by building out the wall on each side of a center window may be perfectly in keeping with the proportions of the room, even if this work was done in recent years. Architectural critic Calvert Vaux suggested just such an idea in 1852.

Few are the old houses in which a bathroom or two have not been added to the bedroom floor (or to the bedroom area in a one-story house), commonly off a central hall to serve the whole family. If not included in the original floor plan, as the bathroom was in most late-Victorian dwellings, such a facility was often installed without disrupting the structural character of a house: back passageways, large walk-in closets, even dressing rooms have been adapted for this purpose. Unless the space found today is totally inadequate for the purpose or was designed in an awkward manner—in whatever period—it is best to leave what *is* well enough alone. Fixtures can be changed fairly easily, as can wall coverings and lighting devices, without undertaking the very costly structural alterations necessary when rerouting pipes. But absolutely to be avoided in the modernization process necessary for any old house is the sacrifice of space integral to a bedroom's proportions and historic character or style.

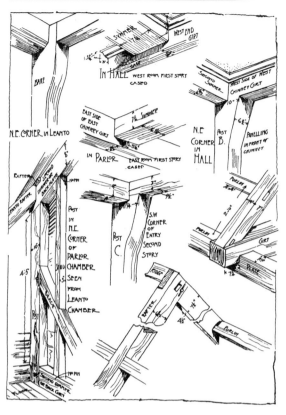

Framing details, Thomas Painter House, West Haven, Connecticut, c. 1685. All the framing in this early house is of oak, and much of this is visible in the interior walls. The decision of whether to case in or to plaster over such structural members as beams, girts, corner posts, braces, and plates was often an economic one in the days of early settlement. The exposed ceiling-beam look of today, which is considered quintessentially "period," has been exaggerated in the remodeling of old houses. Although such elements as beams or joists may have been exposed originally, their enclosure was often accomplished within a short period of time after the house was built.

Back bedroom, private residence, southeastern Massachusetts, added c. 1725 to a 1715 dwelling; the photograph dates from c. 1900. Two beams have been left exposed for over 250 years in the ceiling of this bedroom, a chamber relegated to the use of children during most of that time. For another view of this room, see page 45. Pictures of the much more sophisticated principal bedroom are shown on pages 43-44.

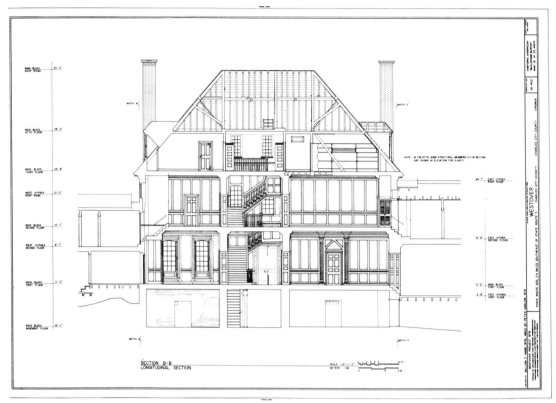

Above: Sectional view of main block, "Westover," near Charles City, Virginia, 1729-35. Built of brick in Flemish bond, the William Byrd II dwelling far outdistanced in building technology the commonplace house of the period. Fine wood paneling and detailing were originally found in Westover's second or chamber floor, although it was not further embellished with elaborate ceiling ornamentation or marble mantels of the sort found in the rooms below. *Left:* "Interior of Bed-room in the Gothic Style," from A. J. Downing, *The Architecture of Country Houses* (1850). Very few examples of the Gothic style in American domestic architecture survive today in contrast to the large numbers of houses in the Greek Revival and Italianate styles. And even fewer bedrooms featuring a vaulted ceiling with ornamental plaster beams are to be found. As Downing lamented, "The ceilings of bed-rooms in country houses in this style are, for the most part, flat, and only relieved by a simple Gothic cornice." Most Americans sought picturesque expression in more simple and cosmetic ways.

A wall may seem hardly worthy of study, but its depth, texture, and decoration can be crucial to a successful restoration project, and these elements differ from period to period. The exterior second-floor walls in an early New England clapboard are likely to be no more than seven-feet high and of studs and clay infill covered simply with whitewash; those in a bedroom of an 1860s Italianate or Second Empire house are higher, probably hollow, and formed of lathe over studs and a strong mortar. First-floor walls in 19th-century dwellings were sometimes brick- or rubble-filled for purposes of insulation and then given several coats of plaster; little attempt was made to so protect the second floor, and often what was then called a "hard finish" of plaster was considered too costly.

Unlike walls, which differ only by degree from one house to another, windows from one period differ dramatically from windows of another. Casement windows were the standard until the early 1700s, and the panes were likely to be small and diamond-shaped. Window glass was a luxury throughout much of the Colonial period and also later on the Western frontier. The bedroom floor or area was likely to have been supplied with fewer windows than the main area of the house in the early years of settlement. Beginning in the early 18th century there was a steady increase in the use of double-hung English sash, the upper member of which was fixed in place. In the typical new Georgian Colonial or remodeled center-hall structure, first- and second-floor windows were arranged to present a symmetrical, classical façade. The windows of the second floor, however, were generally smaller than those of the first, and each sash often contained an equal number of lights—six, eight, nine, depending on the size of the house—rather than an unequal

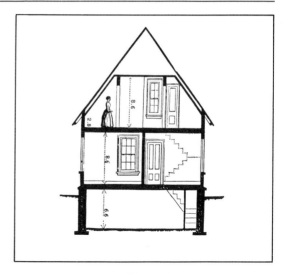

Top: Sectional view of a Carpenter Gothic cottage with three bedrooms on the second floor, from *Village and Farm Cottages* (1855) by Henry W. Cleaveland, William Backus, and Samuel D. Backus. The very steep pitch of the roof allowed for maximum use of the second floor without resort to dormers. At the same time, the interior must have been quite gloomy. In modern restoration and renovation work, roof panels or skylights can often be used to open up the space without destroying its basic lines. *Above:* Wash basin and alcove, front bedroom, Moore-Cunningham House, Boise, Idaho, late 19th century, as photographed in the 1930s. With the installation of indoor plumbing, the ceramic basin and pitcher and the commode on which they stood began to disappear from the bedroom. Not all rooms, however, were without the convenience of an area in which to wash. Yet another utilitarian feature of the 19th-century bedroom was the transom. It provided for the flow of air at night when doors were shut.

combination, such as 9 over 6 or 12 over 8, which was used downstairs.

Doors have changed over time from batten or sheathed to paneled affairs. Beginning in the 1860s interior bedroom doors were often removed and replaced with portieres; that leading to the hall usually stayed in place and probably was hung under a transom which allowed for ventilation. Fireplaces were used in some early bedrooms, disappeared in many Victorian rooms, and were then resurrected during the late-19th-century Colonial Revival. Provision for a chimney flue, however, was practically standard during the 19th century, as it had been earlier. Sometimes the chimney projected out into the room, and at other times was flush with an exterior wall, or was made flush by the addition of cupboards and perhaps a tight-winder stairway as in many paneled room ends. Closets were rare in Colonial homes, and, as late as the 1870s and '80s, their function was often supplied by special pieces of furniture such as wardrobes.

Most bedrooms were left fairly open in floor plans, with allowance made for dressing, sleeping, reading, and working. The bay window alcove found in numerous homes from the Gothic Revival to the Second Empire and Queen Anne periods is a pleasant reminder of how graceful a period bedroom can be. It is in the surface decoration of the average old-house bedroom rather than in its structural composition that a period character can be established again.

SCALE   SECTION

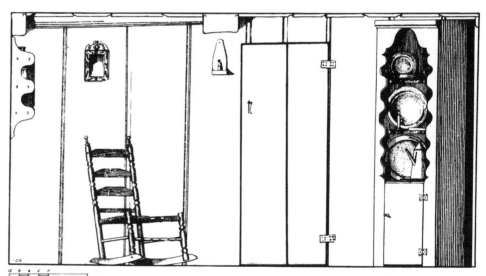

Top (left): Bedroom and study, private residence, California, late 19th century, as photographed in the 1930s. A washstand with running water was provided in this room. The house was a very fashionable one and included what appears to be a solid marble mantel and not one that simulated the expensive material. *Above:* Wall elevation, "Pine-Ceiled Room," Concord Antiquarian Society, Concord, Massachusetts, 1700-25. Vertical tongue-and-groove sheathing on the walls was not at all unusual in the early Colonial period; for it to appear on the ceiling as well was quite extraordinary. At the time, the use of paneling of this sort was less costly and time-consuming in execution than ornamental plasterwork. Simple whitewashed walls and open-beamed ceilings were not considered a charming feature in the fashionable 18th-century dwelling. *Top (right):* Double casement window sash, Connecticut, 17th century. The first window in the common New England dwelling was often nothing more than a wooden shutter or oiled paper; glass was originally used only sparingly. The window took the form of a diamond-paned casement, usually only single and not double, as seen in the photograph on page 13.

No. 4½.

"A neat mantel for a bed-room," from the 1874 catalogue of the Keystone Slate Mantel and Slate Works, Wilson & Miller Co., Philadelphia. A small mantel of this sort was considered appropriate for the average bedroom. A basket grate of the sort illustrated below was available in various sizes from the same company.

Bedroom, Alabama, 19th century, as photographed in the 1930s. Closet space was added to old houses and designed for new homes during the second half of the 19th century. Here the wall has been built out to provide such a convenience. Although both the window at the left and the door to the right have lost their full profile, it would seem unreasonable to remove the addition in a restoration.

Bedroom, H. F. Franklin House, Selma, Alabama, mid-19th century. The bay window alcove could provide a pleasant area for bedroom living. But here, in a photograph from the 1930s, only confusion seems to reign. The wires for the lamp have been threaded through an older gas extension. The unusual placement of the bed suggests that either this was the coolest area of the room or that the bed was used by an invalid.

3.
A Portfolio of Period Bedrooms

The need for a quiet place in which to relax during the day and evening and to pass a restful sleep at night has not changed over the years; neither has the desire to make the bedroom an attractive place lessened any in recent times. Although the bedroom may not be as architecturally distinctive or as ambitiously furnished as the formal areas of an old house, it often displays a more colorful and lavish use of fabrics, paints, and papers. A handsome period bedstead can bring almost any space alive, as can the presence of an open hearth with a wood fire that slowly burns down as the night unwinds. The bedroom—for adult or child—should be a place of repose, for pleasant dreams both day and night.

Most of the bedrooms shown in the following pages are traditional in appointments and quite separate physically from the rest of the house. A few are multipurpose, serving as work areas during the day. These remind us that wherever and whenever pioneers first settled, there were often limited resources available for providing distinct sleeping chambers. A bedroom could also serve as a sitting room or as a place in which to weave and to sew. With increased use of old commercial and industrial buildings for residential purposes today—as illustrated on pp. 39-42—the multipurpose function of living space is being stressed again. The wide variety of interiors shown in the following pages colorfully demonstrates many possibilities of old-house living. Photographed and documented across the country, these rooms provide ample evidence of the imagination being applied to interpreting the past in light of today's needs.

The four-poster rope bed with tester might as well have been made especially for this second-floor New Jersey bedroom. The colonial farmhouse is rigorously regular in its lines and features, the doorways and ceilings clearly defined by unpainted pine framing, and its master bedroom has been left spare in furnishings, "clean" in appearance. Only the gingham check of the bedclothing provides an accent of vivid color. The room is situated at the front of the 1760 house on the left-hand side. Located in rural Monmouth County, the clapboard house originally consisted of only the portion to the left of the center entrance, the other half being added a century later. The present owners have left the siding in its unpainted, weathered condition, a not uncommon practice in coastal areas of New Jersey settled by the English and Dutch.

This bedroom is less formal, but every bit as handsome in composition as the room in the same house shown on the preceding page. It serves as a child's quarters, and the simple but sturdy rope bed is the sort that has held up for generations. Floorcloths are used throughout the house rather than the ubiquitous colonial-style braided ovals more popular today than they were in the 18th century. The woodwork in the room has been decorated with a green-olive buttermilk paint in a matte finish. A chest lies at the foot of the bed, and a massive linen press to the right. Both might be used for the storage of clothing and bedding in a house where closets are few and far between.

Opposite: Only as middle-class families have grown smaller in the 20th century has it been thought necessary to give each child "his own room." Use of one room by several children was common in early American homes; on the frontier, a whole family might have bedded down in the same space. This girls' room in the New Jersey farmhouse has been arranged so that each child has her own clearly defined area. The use of matching beds, Jacquard coverlets, and the floorcloth draw the space together. The furniture is a mixture of 19-century country pieces not at all out of keeping with a house that grew over time from a gable-end chimney dwelling to a full-fledged center-hall residence worthy of a prosperous farmer.

Above: The early colonial houses of the Southwest are as honest and natural in their structural materials as any domestic buildings to be found in North America. The Ignacio de Roybal House, part of a New Mexico Spanish hacienda in existence from at least the mid-18th century, displays the unique blend of Hispanic and Indian craftsmanship so admired today. The use of sun-dried bricks of earth, a Spanish contribution, allowed for the building of massive walls with deep window recesses such as that visible in the bedroom illustrated. From the Indian culture came the tradition of using peeled logs, *vigas,* to support ceilings of split cedar saplings, *latillas.* Interior rooms need little in the way of decoration; plants positioned to capture the slanting rays of sunlight provide an appropriate softening of the interior space. Only the grillwork in the built-in closets at the end of the room displays the elaboration of form common to European architectural styles.

Bedrooms have of course been used for more than rest. Usually found on the second floor of an old house, these areas may offer quiet, undisturbed space for careful and thoughtful work. Although some women may have been trapped in their bedrooms by the household chores of ages past, others — such as the weaver who makes this room (*left*) double as a workshop — produced masterpieces of domestic art in lofty solitude. The materials of the weaver's trade are perched along the beams of the gambrel roof framework out of the way of daily life, but still within reach when needed. The weaver and her husband reassembled a New England Cape (*above*) on a new site in Westport, Massachusetts, and transformed a gable roof to a gambrel to provide more living space on the second floor. A compromise in restoration, yes, but not one that detracts from the basic structural integrity of the house. Other changes were required in flooring and paneling. In each case, old replacement materials were sought which would blend in with the original.

Commercial and industrial buildings in urban areas have been used increasingly for residential purposes. Newport, Rhode Island, is blessed with a series of wharves dating from the early 18th century, one of which (the building at the left) provides space for a duplex apartment above two commercial floors. The mix of residential and business use goes against the grain of 20th-century zoning practice, but was certainly not unusual in earlier times; neither was the use of a living room as a bedroom by night, as illustrated below. The upper floor of the apartment serves as the primary sleeping area, with the living room offering a place for visiting family or friends. Three years were spent in preparing the wharf building for habitation. The walls consisted originally of only clapboards nailed over the studs. As long as the building served as a warehouse, no one would have paid much attention to the wind whistling through. Posts, studs, and weather braces have been left exposed, but now sheet rock has been inserted between.

The second floor of the Newport wharf apartment has as its focal point a giant wood winch used in former days to lift or lower goods through the four floors of the warehouse. (A second view appears on the following page.) There is no use for such an apparatus today, but it is an integral reminder of the building's past, its original function. Machinery such as a wheel or winch can often be used in a most aesthetically pleasing fashion. In this case, the smoothly-finished object separates the floor into two distinct sleeping areas and ties in perfectly with the structural members of the gambrel-roofed loft. In keeping with the informal character of the space, beds are lean and spare. A four-poster would be as out of place here as a Chippendale highboy.

Opposite: Many a simple colonial dwelling was transformed into a Georgian-style center-hall and center-chimney house during the 18th century. This home, in southeast Massachusetts, began in c. 1710-15 as a one-room-deep, two-story dwelling. The center portion was added in c. 1725, and the section to the left in 1830. The bedroom illustrated is found in the earliest part of the house. The present owner has kept the furnishings to a minimum; scatter rugs are used over the wide-plank pine floors, and straight-hanging tab curtains at the windows. This is in keeping with the current belief that early American rooms were rather simple affairs, an argument based on a study of inventories of the period. Only with the rediscovery of the "colonial" style after the Centennial of 1876, did the interpretation become fussy. For another view of this room, furnished in the "colonial" period style as interpreted in the early 1900s, see page 14.

The central position of the fireplace in the colonial-period bedroom is fully illustrated in this second view of the room shown on the previous page. The fireplace is placed against what was the original exterior wall of the house and is surrounded by a raised-panel chimney breast of very simple style. The center panel may have been ornamented at some time.

Among the rooms added to the Massachusetts
house in the 1720s was a second-story back bedroom. There is structural evidence that the space
was divided somewhat differently from the way it
is at present, but there is no doubt that this was
always an informal room, one probably intended
for use by children.

A second-floor room in the Massachusetts house, seen above and on the following page, was added in the 1720s, and served at one time as a bedroom. Today it is no longer needed for this purpose and is used as a sitting room. It is possible that this interior, a great deal more elegant in its appointments than the bedroom illustrated previously, was intended as a fashionable replacement for the earlier room. The very handsome fireplace room end and the corner cupboard display the full flowering of the early Georgian style. The pine doorways are grained in imitation of fine hardwood, a practice that began in the 18th century and continued through the 19th. The floral paper is a late 19th-century addition, multi-colored designs of this sort being impossible to secure in rural New England in the early 1700s. The paper, however, is of a high style and coloring which blends easily with the other decorative elements. The floor in this room has been painted, and appears to have been treated in this manner for many years.

Except for the addition of a bed, perhaps placed against the wall to the left, this room might have been similarly furnished in the 18th century. The table would not have appeared in the center, but rather closer to the fireplace. A bedroom of this sort would have been used for entertaining guests and certainly for quiet domestic pursuits by the lady of the house.

A workingman's cottage in the New Bedford, Massachusetts area, is one of those houses that never changed to any great degree; over a period of many generations, no one could afford to "remodel." One-room deep with an enclosed end chimney, the house was built about 1820. The bedroom occupies most of the second floor of the modest dwelling, a small bathroom and sewing room having been created to one side. In style the three-bay building is typical of those built during the Federal period at the end of the 1700s and in the early years of the 1800s. The main entrance is positioned at one corner of the house, and almost immediately inside are to be found a narrow set of stairs ascending to the upper floor. Here the present owner has created a formal but colorful ambiance in keeping with the neoclassical style of the building. The paper is based on a French resist design used during the colonial and Federal periods when both papers and fabrics were block printed. The convex mirror with spread eagle is a minor decorative element, but an appropriate furnishing in a house of this period.

Opposite: This large Federal-style house in New-port, Rhode Island, was built for speculation by carpenter Samuel Durfee in 1803. It is more sophisticated in its detailing and basic floor plan than the house containing the bedroom shown on the previous page. Except for the kitchen, each of the rooms includes a fancy Adam-style mantel, and all the doors were originally grained. The solid pink shade is a cheerful and appropriate color for the bedroom. Soft color — light blues, greens, and pinks — were fashionable during the Federal period in both fashion and furnishings. Paint was as likely to be used on the walls as paper since the latter was still being produced by hand at considerable expense.

Above: A mid-19th-century Chicago suburban residence in the Italianate style carries little of the Victorian features often thought typical of the period. It is neoclassical in feeling both inside and out, with doors and windows arranged in perfect symmetrical order, their molded casings, as seen here, being simple in composition. The vertical floral paper is like the machine-printed products of over a century ago which home decorators preferred to painted walls. At first the colonial four-poster bed with canopy appears to be a throwback to another era, but such personal furnishings continued to be made and used well into the 19th century in many areas of the country. Even if this were not so, there is no reason why attractive, well-crafted furniture from one stylistic period should not be used in an old house which in its makeup reflects the lives of at least several generations of residents.

Privacy is a requisite for bedrooms. Doors are most often closed at night. The heavy paneled door to the master bedroom in this converted New Mexican mill is a piece of wood sculpture in itself, a handsome example of the art of fine carpentry in the Hispanic tradition. The four-poster bed is similarly unyielding in its monumentality and impressive in its craftsmanship; it forms a very private and secure sleeping alcove. The white coverlet and the printed cotton used on the tester, bed hanging, and dust ruffle provide successful softening effects.

The leisurely amount of space devoted to a master bedroom in a mid-Victorian house is clearly visible in this San Francisco Italianate residence. A special alcove, marked off by a bracketed arch, is set aside for sleeping, leaving the rest of the room free as a sitting and dressing area. Typically, the fireplace is the feature to which the furnishings are oriented. The gracefully-covered marble mantel in the "French" style is found in other rooms as well, including the back bedroom illustrated on the following page. Picture rails or moldings are also used throughout the house.

A back bedroom in the San Francisco Italianate house connects with the front room and probably served as a children's room before a rear wing was added at a later date. The regularity of the space is imaginatively broken by a bay window alcove, a continuation of an extension off the downstairs back parlor. As in that room, the arch is ornamented with plaster brackets at each end. Transoms were originally found over the doors to the hallway leading to the bedrooms, but these have been removed. The solid beige color used on the walls below the picture railings is by no means documented, but it is pleasing and in keeping with the cool, formal spirit of the structure. Both this and the adjoining bedroom were probably originally papered.

Americans arriving in New Mexico during the first half of the 19th century brought with them Eastern architectural styles, including the Greek Revival, which were soon merged with the prevailing Spanish style. Windows and doors in adobe structures were given more elaborate casings; parapets were finished off with an arrangement of bricks in imitation of a dentil molding; as in this room, ceilings were often plastered and square beams used rather than round logs or *vigas*. The style which emerged is known as the Territorial, a style well illustrated by this home in Santa Fe dating from the mid-1800s. To the left may be seen French windows which open up to a balcony overlooking the courtyard; the house also features a two-story porch. The stained-glass panel is a recent addition to the deeply-set window at center.

A Second-Empire town house built in San Francisco in the last quarter of the 19th century has been slowly and intelligently restored to a state of elegance. The façade is distinguished by the Eastlake portico and the handsome columned bay windows. The way in which a bay opened up an interior and provided comfortable space for chairs and a table is indicated in the illustration below of the front master bedroom. The present owner has made every attempt to furnish this and other rooms with period antiques. The étagère to the left of the fireplace, and the dresser to the right, give every appearance of having been made for the bedroom. The rose wallpaper is an early 20th-century pattern. Wall-to-wall carpeting is used just as it probably was in the late 1800s; the solid color preferred in the 1980s, however, is a substitute for a Victorian floral pattern.

The back bedroom in the San Francisco house is also handsomely furnished with appropriate antiques. Here, too, as in the previous room, a gasolier is used for lighting. Lace curtains filter the light; at one time such delicate textiles were often used as underliners for heavy draperies. Of brocade, silk, velvet, or other woven materials, these elaborate hangings are expensive to reproduce faithfully and difficult to maintain. Many contemporary home owners choose to do without them. Unless their past use can be documented in a particular house, there is no compelling reason to reproduce such window hangings.

Houses that are small and easy to heat are appreciated with a new fervor today. Most old houses are not elaborate sprawling buildings, but modest and often undistinguished structures. North America's major cities are full of such dwellings, primarily row houses built for working-class families. Such cottages in the Queen Anne style are the special pride of San Francisco. Highly ornamented on the outside, they are relatively restrained in interior decor. The average floor plan consists of one floor with a double-parlor, an entrance hall, kitchen, and bath. A bedroom may be found here as well since many of the houses were built without provision for a separate bedroom floor, the top level being only an unfinished attic. The bedroom in this Queen Anne cottage is found on the main living floor, behind a back parlor and next to the kitchen. Only the lighting fixture and plant stand to the right provide any clue to the period of the interior; the woodwork has been painted ever since the house was built in 1899.

Prosperous individuals could afford much more elaborate Queen Anne style dwellings. The Hanger House, built for a Little Rock businessman, dates from the 1870s, but took its present form—double the size of the original—in 1889. The master bedroom is situated at the front of the house, and is here seen from an adjoining child's room. Both a door and portiere are used to separate the rooms, doubling privacy and insulation from cold.

The sleeping end of the Hanger House master bedroom is seen in this view. The woodwork used
through most of the house is of cypress stained to
approximate golden oak; the crowned corner
moldings of the windows are found in many Queen
Anne homes and are among the details sometimes
called "Eastlake" after the English designer and architect whose highly turned and bracketed work
was as popular in North America as in Great Brit-
ain. The Renaissance Revival bed is of an earlier,
but complimentary, style. Opposite the bed is the
sitting area of the room, and, to the left, a pleasant
bay alcove.

Matching oak beds define this children's room in the Hanger House as impeccably Victorian in form. The use of lace bedspreads echoes the similar treatment given to window hangings throughout the house. Modern art does not at all detract from the structural and decorative harmony of the space. In fact, it gives the room a definite character which sets it apart from many period museum rooms in which mannequins and furnishings are artifically frozen in time.

An early one-room-deep adobe structure lies at the heart of a ranch restored and enlarged in the late 1920s by architect John Gaw Meem. Located in the Rio Grande Valley village of Los Ranchos de Albuquerque, New Mexico, the complex of farm buildings is one of the most gracious and impressive to be found in the Southwest. The child's bedroom illustrated is part of the center residence built around a *placita* or interior courtyard. Nearly all of the rooms in this square complex, one-third of which comprises the original building, open up on the courtyard. While one can walk from room to room around the square, it is much easier and more pleasant to cross the central open space. Architect Meem used old materials and methods in most of the addition, including the door seen here, and the present owners have furnished the ranch home in a style sympathetic to the building's character. The main entrance to the building is seen in the exterior photograph.

Above: The master bedroom of the Rio Grande ranch lies at one corner of the 1920s addition. Its large double sash windows and generally modern structural appearance reflect the former owner's desire for a contemporary bedroom secluded from the rest of the house, yet open as much as possible to the out-of-doors. Little attempt was made to invest the room with period details in keeping with the style the structure emulates. In this respect it is typical of many interiors remodeled or designed during the first decades of the 20th century in the Spanish Colonial-revival style throughout the United States.

Left: The Colonial Revival style of English derivation gained great favor in the Eastern half of the country from the 1890s through the 1930s. In its earliest phases, the style was an admixture of Queen Anne, Elizabethan, and Georgian; gradually, the more restrained neoclassical style of the Beaux Arts school gained the ascendancy. The Wait House, a residence in Little Rock, was built in c. 1897-99 and combines Queen Anne features with those of the Beaux Arts. This mixture is seen in the molded door casing to the right, with one corner block visible, and in the decorative terra-cotta fireplace surround. The owners of the home have skillfully combined late Victorian and turn-of-the-century furnishings and have equipped the rooms with light fixtures that provide either gas or electric light.

4.
The Architectural Furnishings: Millwork, Plasterwork, and Hardware

In speaking historically of the architectural furnishings of a bedroom—woodwork, plaster ornamentation, mantels, hardware, shutters—only bedchambers occupied by adults are of serious concern. Until the late-19th century secondary bedrooms for children were not decorated with much care except in the homes of the very wealthy. Lewis Allen, a popular writer on rural architecture, wrote in 1852 that "If, to a single parlor, or spare bedchamber a little ornamental work be permitted, let even that be in moderation. . . ." Although this advice was not always followed in ensuing years—particularly during what Lewis Mumford has termed the brown decades (1865-95), when seemingly every projection in a room had to be draped—the average family's pocketbook, however, dictated that rooms for sleeping be modest.

The first separate bedchambers of 17th- or early-18th-century dwellings were simply whitewashed spaces in which beams and other elements in the house's framing, such as posts, weather braces, and collars, were exposed. Ceilings in formal "living rooms" were the first to have lathe and plaster; bedrooms came later. Most of the early bedrooms were not supplied with fireplaces until the 18th century. At this time, a more sophisticated approach to the finishing of the room came into fashion. By the 1720s, as illustrated on pages 43-47, the Georgian mode was becoming established in the colonies. Paneled room ends were by no means unknown in a separate 17th-century bedroom, but now raised paneling was being specified to simulate pilasters and bases, and elaborate moldings were called for to define the dado, wall panels, and cornice. A frieze running under the cornice was sometimes considered essential to the overall design and became an important element in Federal-style decoration during the late 1700s. Paneled walls were, of course, an exception in most houses. More common were roughly-plastered walls with a base and a chair rail defining the dado area and the rail and a cornice defining the wall panel area. Wainscoting was usually employed only in the principal rooms.

Doors and windows were given special attention during the high-Colonial period by the application of well-articulated casings, although these rarely were capped with pediments and architraves of the sort used in more formal rooms. The wood used in the bedroom for casings and moldings was most often white pine. It was frequently painted in various deep hues which contrasted sharply with the whitewashed or plastered walls. The white-painted woodwork thought in the 1890s to be particularly "Colonial" is more reminiscent of the

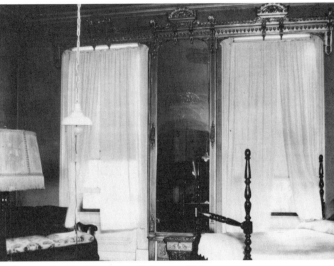

"Cornices for Beds or Windows" from George Hepplewhite's *The Cabinet-Maker and Upholsterer's Guide* (third edition, 1794). The practice of draping windows in the same manner as beds in fashionable 18th-century interiors brought about another use for the cornice. Draperies could not be simply hung from rods or poles, but had to be tucked behind an ornamental device.

Bedroom, Smith Mansion, Alabama, 19th century, as photographed in the 1930s. Elaborate window cornices were forgotten to a large extent in the early 1800s but by the mid-century gilded plaster and wooden fabrications were popular in high-style homes. The use of a pier mirror between two windows was a common practice, and the extension of the cornice to form a single overarching decorative element was a device frequently employed.

early 19th-century room and may not be Colonial at all.

Provision was also made in the Georgian-style bedroom for fireplaces and mantels, the latter complementing in composition the basic scheme of the walls — base, pilaster, and cornice or architrave. Fireplace openings were smaller than those used in the parlor and kitchen and gradually decreased in size over succeeding years. A fire was not maintained all through the day or night in the room and there was little need for the elaborate fireplace apparatuses required elsewhere. The stoves and grates that came to be used after the mid-1700s were also smaller in size.

Interior shutters had been common since the 1600s. Among the earliest types were sliding affairs made of wooden planks which could be drawn across a window. In the 18th century paneled and hinged models which could be folded back at each side began to replace the sliders. These, too, were solid panels, often raised, and not the louvered sort used in the 19th century. Since curtains were often not used in the bedroom for windows, such shutters provided privacy at night and, in the absence of storm windows, helped to cut down on drafts.

Bedrooms during the early 19th century remained quite spare. The type of ornamental plastering considered fashionable in a high-style parlor or sitting room — ceiling centerpieces and stuccoed friezes — was simply not called for in the bedchamber. Brackets came into play to define bay window alcoves, but for the most part, ornamentation was applied only in the form of paint and paper. If ceilings needed decoration, for instance, this was likely to take the form of a printed paper. The one archi-

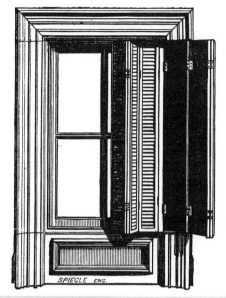

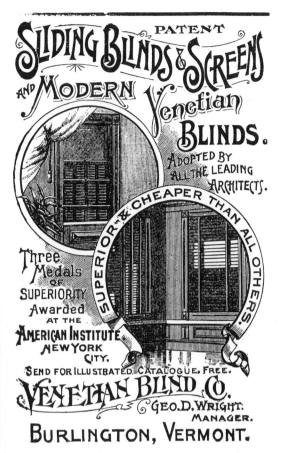

Top (left): Pocket shutters, made by Wright & Thompson, Elizabeth, New Jersey, from an advertisement in *Bicknell's Village Builder* (1872). During the Victorian era solid or louvered shutters, also known as blinds, were used as often inside a house as on the exterior. Sometimes they took the place of curtains or of draperies. *Top (right):* Venetian blinds and sliding blinds, Venetian Blind Co., Burlington, Vermont, 1898. The use of wooden Venetian blinds began in the 18th century, but the practice did not assume widespread popularity until the early 1900s. Sliding blinds were yet another form of shutters preferred by many Victorian housewives because they were easier to use than the vertical models. *Above:* Plaster ceiling ornament, Bragg-Mitchell House, Mobile, Alabama, 1847, Thomas James, architect. Fine work of this sort was usually saved for the parlor or dining room, but was also specified by architects for the principal bedroom. When fixtures were electrified, it was often the practice to thread the wiring through the existing gas pipe so that the centerpiece or rosette could be left undisturbed.

tectural element that might carry some sort of applied ornamentation was the mantel. The Adamesque form, rigidly classical, was often embellished with composition or plaster festoons and the acanthus; in the Greek Revival period of the 1820s through the '40s, mantel decoration featured the anthemion and fret and key motives.

In the 1840s a preference for natural wood tones in furniture and woodwork became dominant. With the arrival of lavish French Rococo forms came a corresponding interest in such fine woods as black walnut and mahogany stained a dark brownish red. So-called "French polish," a varnish introduced in the 1820s, could be used to protect woodwork for some time. A. J. Downing in *The Architecture of Country Houses* (1850) advised the use of such a finish for pine, which he claimed gave the effect of "the plainer portions" of oak or black walnut" and the "effect of time to the actual grain of the wood." Several generations of Victorians agreed with his judgment that "There is something warm and comfortable in the aspect of a room stained in this way, and when there is any scantiness of furniture it helps to give the apartment a finished appearance."

With the widespread use of suites of cottage furniture, there was less and less a likelihood that a bedroom would display a barren look after the mid-19th century. It was possible, however, to lack the architectural detailing considered traditional in the 18th century. Cornices were often omitted in house plans of the 1870s through the '90s. In their place might be wallpaper borders below which would run a molding or rail for hanging pictures. Clarence Cook in *The House Beautiful* (1881) called these moldings "picture strips" and counseled that they were to be found "in all our picture-frame shops and the hooks that belong with them. . . ."

The kinds of hardware used for doors and windows in the past seem rather extravagant today by comparison. Iron, the common material for such fittings in the Colonial-style house, continued to be used in the average home in cast form, but solid brass — previously found only in the houses of the wealthy — found special favor with the Victorians. Brass hardware was often stamped with ornate designs. The great variety of Colonial forms — strap, butterfly, and H and HL hinges being among the most common — slowly disappeared from view in the 19th century. Simple butt hinges took their place. Although mass produced, they nonetheless dress up any solid door or cabinet, and this was the intent of the Victorian homemaker. Although the Victorian bedroom was basically a utilitarian space lacking in architectural detailing, it was not one without small touches of elegance.

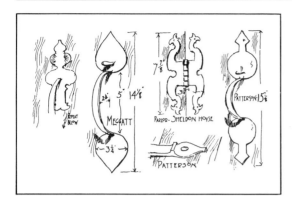

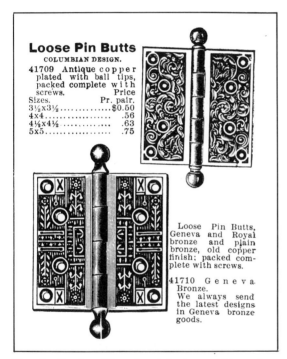

Top: A collection of iron thumb latches and hinges from late-17th- and early-18th-century Connecticut houses.

Above: Loose pin butt hinges, from the 1895 Montgomery Ward & Co. catalogue. Copper plated or of bronze, such extremely utilitarian pieces were given a finish worthy of solid doors and other objects to which they were attached. The use of a loose pin made the removal of doors much easier when moving large pieces of furniture from room to room.

Top: Fluted door knob and escutcheon from the Dr. Henry Genet Taylor House, Camden, New Jersey, 1886, Wilson Eyre, Jr., architect. Although most hardware used in the home during the late 19th century was inexpensively stamped, craftsmen could still supply such handsome ornamental pieces as that illustrated here.

Above: A gas bracket, termed "Pretty by Day or Night" from *The House Beautiful* (1881) by Clarence Cook. Gas fixtures grew more and more elaborate during the 19th century, and some critics found them grotesque. Cook advocated a return to adaptations of the simpler forms used for candles, and his advice was widely followed.

5.
Paints, Papers, and Fabrics

Lacking architectural distinction, the bedroom has been a prime candidate for the kinds of decorative materials — paints, papers, textiles — which cover up or embellish an interior. Of all the secondary spaces in the house, what was termed in the 19th century the "Mother's room" or the principal chamber for the adults was often the most decorated. Considered a quiet, comfortable sanctuary from the workaday troubles of the real world, this room was a place to indulge the fanciful, the little personal frills and flounces. This was a room that not only suggested ease in its appointments, but encouraged relaxation.

In the beginning of settlement it was difficult to provide such a sanctuary from the outside world. But even in the 17th century the bedstead suggested something of the privacy, security, and comfort which was to surround the activity of sleeping. "Variety in bed hangings," Abbott Lowell Cummings has written in *Bed Hangings, A Treatise on Fabrics and Styles in the Curtaining of Beds, 1650-1850,* "seems to have been the spice of the Colonial home." The paraphernalia used to define and decorate the four-poster was extensive and, as suggested, varied in form, material, and decoration. The bedsteads sometimes considered "Colonial" today — one with an arched canopy — was not, in fact popular until the late 18th century. This form, known popularly as a French field bed, supplanted but did not entirely replace use of the traditional Colonial flat-top bedstead with a base, head cloth and curtains which drew around the sides and end, and a valance and tester. Materials used in the 17th and 18th centuries for such hangings were calico, linen, linsey-woolsey, say, chintz, dimity, and woolen fabrics like harrateen and cheney. A considerable amount of material was required for the curtains, and such luxurious fabrics as silk were rarely used.

Bed hangings were not indulged for their handsomeness alone, but because they served a functional purpose in keeping the occupants of the bed warm and secluded. Later, as the need for warmth and privacy was met in other ways, hangings began to change. Foot curtains were the first to go, and, in the words of Cummings, "there was at the same time a shrinking of the once functional curtain from full length to a mere decorative appendage or cascade." The trend of draping for ornamental rather than functional purposes was to continue throughout the 19th century as heating technology advanced.

Windows in most early Colonial bedrooms were without curtains, there being little material available for decoration. Interior shutters provided the best possible

Above: Southeast bedroom, Black House, Ellsworth, Maine, 1824-27. Everything in this room suggests comfort. Each piece of furniture is covered in some manner. The bed hangings are elaborate, and the bed features a heavily-draped cornice. In keeping with the more subdued aesthetic of the early 19th century—in contrast to the stuffed exuberance of the late Victorian period—the decor is a model of restraint. The windows are not laden down with layers of fabric, nor is a cornice featured at the top of each. The wall-to-wall carpeting is fitting for a well-appointed home of the perod. *Above (right):* A bedstead termed a "square Gothic," as illustrated in *Beautiful Homes* (1878) by Henry T. Williams and Mrs. C. S. Jones. Such a model became popular earlier in the century and always featured headboards and footboards of equal height and finial decorations. The drapery of Swiss cotton edged with lace was considered a "charming finish." *Right:* Iron bedstead, with canopy, from *Hints on Household Taste* (1878) by Charles L. Eastlake. Beds of iron, brass, and imitation bronze were introduced in the first half of the 19th century. Eastlake's model differed substantially by the use of a canopy and curtains. "Many people now-a-days prefer, on sanitary grounds," he wrote, "to sleep, through the winter as well as the summer, in beds without hangings of any kind. It is difficult to conceive, however, that in a well-ventilated apartment, a canopy and head curtains can be at all prejudicial to health, and it is certain that they may be made to contribute not a little to the picturesqueness of a modern bed-room."

protection from the elements. The openings in the walls, of course, were at first small, and to decorate them with textiles would have been a superfluous act. As the size of windows increased, so did the use of hangings. As Downing wrote in 1850, "Next to carpets, which are universal in all but the dwellings of the very poor in America, nothing 'furnishes' a room so much as curtains to the windows." Downing's emphasis on the desirability of curtains suggests that their use during the 19th century was not quite so common as we believe today; contemporary paintings and prints tell the same story. Interior shutters continued in use throughout the 1800s, sometimes with simple hangings. Among the most popular of these were sash curtains, now known as cafe curtains or half-curtains, which covered the lower moveable sash, the top sash being fixed in place. The curtains were often made of homespun or cotton in solid colors or prints and they were hung in a straight line by strings or cord. Another form of curtain popular in sophisticated homes in the first half of the 19th century was the festoon which could be drawn up and down in the manner of an Austrian shade. Such a curtain, however, was less likely to be found in the bedroom than in the parlor or dining room.

Fancier curtains in use in fashionable homes of the Victorian period were those that could be tied back at the sides of the windows. "The history of window hanging in the 19th century," William Seale has explained, "is dominated by curtains that are tied back, from the crimson silk of 1810, bordered in galloon and tied back waist-high, to the white lace of the 1860s tied back knee-high, making deep, sweeping folds." The fabrics used for curtains became more and more elaborate during the first half of the 19th century. Added to these

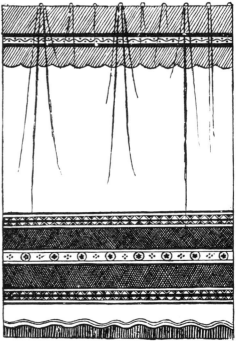

C. HANCOCK. ELECTR PHOTO

Embroidered portiere curtains from *Hints on Household Taste*. These designs by C. Heaton were strongly recommended by Eastlake. Horizontal banding of this sort came into fashion in the 1870s and '80s; fine embroidery work was encouraged by advocates of domestic arts and crafts.

hangings were such appendages as liners, cornices, lambrequins, and draperies. As more and more of the outside world filtered in through the undivided or minimally-divided sash of the Victorian house, the greater seemed to be the housewife's effort to shut out the light, the dirt, and the noise.

Liners were useful in protecting fine fabrics from the effects of the sun and, until the mid-19th century, were usually made of muslin; lace was standard until the early 1900s. Draperies, as distinct from curtains, served no practical purpose. They were fixed appendages. Lambrequins, hung in great scallops, were the most elaborate of these hangings to be found in the well-appointed bedroom. Quite often they were enclosed at the top in an ornate cornice made of wood and covered with the same or a similar fabric. In the second half of the century Swiss lace was used for curtains as well as for liners, and in many modest homes only this material, hung from a simple rod, was to be found at the window. Such curtains were sufficiently patterned to screen out the outside and were often used along with a roller blind or shade. Known since the 1700s, these shades were standard in many homes. Early in the 1800s a fashion developed of painting shades with decorations which created an interesting luminescent effect when struck by light; these were known as transparencies. Their use faded from popularity late in the century.

During the 1890s and the early 20th century the reaction to the overdraping and stuffing of interiors was overwhelming. Heavy draperies and curtains were considered unhealthful and a fire hazard. Out went even the lace, to be replaced by theatrical gauze, muslin, or what was known as the glass curtain—a sheer, unpatterned

Top: Nottingham lace curtains, from the Montgomery Ward & Co. catalogue, 1895. These were available in white or ecru, each curtain measuring 3½ yards long, 47 inches wide, with a single taped border. Home decorators search far and wide today for such materials which were commonplace during most of the 19th century. The price for a pair was $1.38. *Above:* Bedroom, Alabama, late 19th century. In many homes curtains of very sheer material—muslin or cotton—were used in at least the summer months. The material was very cheap, too cheap many critics thought. Muslin was also used for bed hangings, especially in the Southern states.

material which hung directly against the sash. Flounces and frills did not, however, disappear altogether. One of the most popular of the curtain forms popular during the Colonial Revival of the 1890s and early 20th century was the "Priscilla," thought then as being of antique origin. Wharton and Codman were of a different opinion at the turn of the century: "Lingerie effects do not combine well with architecture, and the more architecturally a window is treated, the less it need be dressed up in ruffles."

Fabrics or textiles were used elsewhere in both the 18th- and 19th-century bedroom, first for floor coverings and then as upholstery and slipcovers. It is clear now that carpets of any sort were almost unknown during the early years of settlement. Orientals, referred to as "Turkeys" in Colonial inventories, were few in number and, where found, were not trod underfoot but used as table coverings or hangings. The "ruggs" of the Colonial period were likely to be bed coverings, early counterpanes. In the bedrooms a handmade scatter rug, hooked or braided, might appear on each side of the bed and before the hearth if a room was supplied with a fireplace. Carpeting and large-size rugs were expensive commodities in Colonial America, and, in large part, had to be imported. Once material of this sort began to be manufactured in the United States in any quantity during the early 1800s, the fashion for them spread very rapidly among the populace. Venetian carpeting—a striped, non-pile machine-produced textile—was extremely popular in the 1820s and '30s and continued to be used in rural areas for bedrooms, halls, and stairways throughout the 19th century.

The vogue for wall-to-wall carpeting continued through the 19th century, but there was an increased appreciation of large carpets or rugs which allowed for a narrow band of wood flooring to be exposed on all sides of a room. Charles Eastlake summed up the feeling of many sophisticated Victorians in this regard: "the practice of entirely covering up the floor . . . is contrary to the first principles of decorative art, which require that the nature of construction, so far as is possible, should always be revealed, or at least indicated, by the ornament which it bears." The use of wall-to-wall carpeting was seen as a veritable admission by Americans that their floors were badly made. With increasing use of hardwood flooring, however, there was less reason to cover the entire surface. Wiltons, Brussels, and Scotch or ingrain carpets and oriental rugs were among those used in at least the principal bedroom in better homes. By the late 19th century, however, the use of carpets in a bedroom was under attack by the hygienists and Colonial Revival aficionados. In *The House Beautiful* Clarence Cook stated the case:

If carpets are not desirable in the living-rooms of the house, much less are they desirable in the bedrooms. . . . A good rug at either side of the bed, and one of the long narrow rugs stretched at the foot of the bed between it and the fireplace, and reaching from one side of the room to the other, will cover the floor generously and will not hinder the thorough sweeping and cleaning of the room.

Textiles were by no means the only kinds of floor covering used in the bedroom in the past. Floorcloths, an early form of linoleum, were produced in large and small sizes in England from the mid-18th century and in the United States from at least the early 1800s. Painted and heavily varnished pieces of canvas, they were useful in all rooms and continued for some time to be placed over carpeting in dining rooms and hallways to catch spills and take heavy wear. Straw matting also performed a useful function. Known variously as Canton or Madras matting, it was used in the bedroom primarily during the summer months.

In discussing the decoration of floors, one inevitably turns to the most common of methods and mediums—paint. In the early 19th century floors, if decorated at all, were painted a solid color or were spattered or stenciled. This was particularly the case in rural areas, although the extent of the itinerant stencil artist's trips has probably been exaggerated by modern commentators who give the impression that nearly every 19th-century farmhouse was visited at one time by either a traveling portrait painter or a stenciler. When it came to decorating floors, the artistic means were probably found much closer to home.

The same situation applied to the decoration of walls and ceilings, with the home owner or a local painter/decorator doing the work. In this regard it is useful to remember that until the time when ready-mixed paints were available (dated as the 1870s by the experts), paint was not an inexpensive commodity to be lavished in every corner of the house. As used in the average Colonial-period dwelling, it was probably reserved for woodwork, the walls remaining simply whitewashed or wood-paneled. In the 19th century the practice of kalsomining walls became prevalent. This process consisted of mixing sizing with a watercolor wash. A number of shades could be effected at a cost estimated by A. J. Downing in 1850 to be one-third that of oil paint.

Downing also strongly urged the use of wallpapers. Ever since the introduction of power presses in the late 1840s, papering a room or a portion of it was a less expensive proposition than painting it. "We confess," he wrote, "a strong partiality for the use of paper-hangings for covering the walls of all cottages." Downing recommended as well their use in more ambitious farmhouses and villas. The utility of papers was without question. Mass produced, they were available in rolls sufficient in length for any possible wall; unlike the earlier hand-blocked versions, most of which were imported, little or no artistry was needed to insure a proper repeat of pattern. In addition, a paper could be laid over the surface of almost any wall regardless of the surface's finish. A good paint job required a hard finish of plaster.

Some of the earliest papers were completely plain except for the printing of such architectural details as panels, friezes, and cornices. These were appropriate for the classical interiors found in many Federal and Greek Revival homes built during the first several decades of the 19th century. Others were flocked in imitation of textile wall coverings. Fresco papers simulated the effect of complicated plaster ornamentation. Until the 1870s, French designs dominated the market, but these were made in America for the most part. From the 1850s these were of strong color combinations—blue and brown, red and brown—which reflected the prevailing Rococo Revival taste. Papers of the succeeding post-Civil War Renaissance Revival were more restrained and featured smaller motifs. In matters of proportion, the mid-Victorian taste was "vertical" in that it favored the piling up of form upon form in the French fashion. Ceilings were high, and paper printed in long paneled patterns climbed the walls in an almost endless manner. Only with the return to favor of English-style papers in the mid-'70s was there expressed a new appreciation of the classical division of dado, fill (or horizontal) panel, and cornice. Since papers were so inexpensive, two

Top (left): Design for a carpet, Henderson & Co., Durham, England, 1851. England supplied the needs of many American customers seeking quality floor coverings well into the 20th century. Although production grew rapidly in the United States from the 1840s on, English designers and textile craftsmen were remarkably attuned to foreign demands for new and colorful patterns and weaves. *Top (right):* "Sleepy Hollow" chair and ottoman for the "afflicted," from *Beautiful Homes.* Fringe, tassels, and an afghan embellished what was already a rotund upholstered confection. The stumpy appearance was intentional; the weary could drop easily in the heavily-padded contrivance. Almost every home had at least one such comfortable piece; it was often found in "mother's" room.

Above: Stenciled bedroom wall design, Hanson House, Windham Center, Maine, 1803. The designs are attributed to the most famous and accomplished of itinerant New England artists, Moses Eaton. Decoration of this sort was especially popular in the Northeast during the early 19th century.

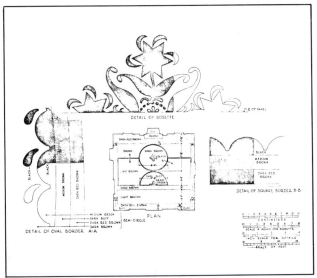

Stencil border along hallway walls (*top*) and a painted floor design (*above*), "The Lindens," built in Danvers, Massachusetts, 1754, and moved to Washington, D.C., in the 1930s. These stencil designs may have been executed in the 18th century. Both are found on the second or chamber floor. In the 19th century expensive French Dufour & Leroy papers were applied to the walls of the formal rooms downstairs. To find both sophisticated imported papers and stencil-work today in the same period dwelling is extremely unusual.

or three (or more) different patterns could be used to imitate the architectural divisions.

By the late 19th century many decorators were thoroughly sick of wallpaper. As a replacement for wood paneling and moldings, plasterwork, and wall hangings in the grand European manner, wallpaper was now deemed unsatisfactory. "Besides being objectionable on sanitary grounds," Wharton and Codman grumped, "they are inferior as a wall-decoration to any form of treatment, however simple, that maintains, instead of effacing, the architectural lines of a room." The lines, perhaps, of a Beaux Arts town house or a Georgian Colonial dwelling, but not a vast majority of the homes built after the Civil War. Nevertheless, papers did fall into disfavor, and in their places more and more home owners of the 20th century turned to the use of paint for a fresh new look.

6.
Furnishing the Period Bedroom

In addition to its obvious utility, furniture has always been used to establish a stylistic flavor, an impression of fashionable good taste. In the words of A. J. Downing, "tasteful furniture is simply, furniture remarkable for agreeable and harmonious lines and forms, well adapted to the purpose in view. Furniture in good taste is characterized by its being designed in accordance with certain recognized styles, and intended to accord with apartments in the same style." This ideal, perhaps workable to some degree in a brand-new house or for a public museum, is difficult to achieve in the average old house. It is, indeed, questionable whether Downing's approach is the right one for the person attempting the restoration of a private home. As mentioned earlier, the documentary evidence from the past—in the form of photographs, prints, and drawings—suggests that the harmony of style held to be ideal was rarely achieved. Rather, furnishings were generally eclectic and were representative of at least several generations. Even when building a new house, a family has always been likely to carry along treasures from the old. Perhaps a better guideline for furnishing might be that of seeking harmony in scale, material, and quality of workmanship.

Only in the very earliest Colonial-period dwelling was one likely to find a consistent style at work. Even then, forms decidedly medieval, the oak wainscot chair for instance, were likely to be found alongside more modern pieces such as a William and Mary walnut lowboy.

The high four-poster is probably the most popular and well documented of period beds. It is perhaps not generally known, however, that many Colonial homes had only one or none of this type, and depended instead on the use of low-post forms or even more primitive substitutes as rushes or pine branches arranged on the floor to form a mattress. Even in the great houses of the 18th century, what is now called a hired man's bed—a low-poster —often served equally well for the children. A feather mattress was a prized possession, but one of straw was far more common.

The canopied field bed is often confused with the traditional four-poster with hangings which derived from the Tudor bedstead of oak. The tester frame in the field bed, however, is arched and usually supported by vase-shaped turnings rather than square or evenly-turned posts. Either the older-style four-poster with hangings that enclosed the bed or the somewhat later French field bed might have been made of maple, walnut, or mahogany, although it is likely that the field bed would have been made of the last-named wood.

Bedroom, "Camden Place," near Port Royal, Virginia, 1856-59, N.G. Starkwether, architect. The original mid-19th-century bedroom suite is still in use in this room. The 18th-century Chippendale looking glass is probably a later addition. Mixing of furnishing styles can work in many period interiors; in this case, however, there is a radical difference in style and usage. The dissonant effect is heightened by the placement of the glass over a marble-topped washstand.

In high-style households of the 19th century, French styles in furniture prevailed. The sleigh bed or crown bed, positioned along a wall with equally high headboard and footboard and a canopy draped across its full length, was one of the first popular fashions. Later, the towering half-tester bed designed by Prudent Mallard, and John Belter's rosewood semi-sleigh bed—both without any draping—were recognized for their fine craftsmanship. The Victorian Renaissance walnut bed of 1855-75, termed Eastlake, with an elaborately paneled high headboard displaying applied molding, achieved similar recognition. It was widely copied in cheaper woods by commercial furniture makers.

Metal beds of wrought iron were introduced in France in the 18th century, and steel came into use there early in the 1800s. It wasn't until the introduction of cast iron and brass models in the United States in the second half of the 1800s, however, that metal construction became a real alternative to wood. Much more likely to have been used by the average American was a low wooden bed composed of equally high head- and footboards and spool-turned spindles and rails, or a simple high-post bed with a curved headboard and no draperies of any sort. Many of the common beds were sold in suites containing as many as eight or ten pieces; such ensembles could be purchased quite cheaply if made of pine or maple.

The critics of late-19th-century interior design regularly railed against the work of assembly-line manufacturers of parlor and

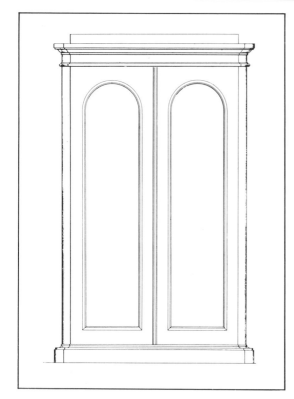

Above: Wardrobe, from George Hepplewhite's *The Cabinet-Maker and Upholsterer's Guide* (1787), and *below:* wardrobe from Blackie and Son's *The Cabinet Maker's Assistant* (1853). Both pieces have a place in period bedrooms. Hepplewhite's classic design is well suited to a late-Colonial or Federal-period room; that of Blackie & Son, which resembles an armoire more than it does a linen press, would be right for most mid- to late-19th-century interiors.

bedroom sets. Charles Eastlake denounced Grand Rapids' drive for profit at the expense of quality, and Clarence Cook in turn decried what he termed "Eastlake" in 1881:

There needs today to be a protest made by some one against the mechanical character of our decoration. . . . Immense furniture mills are set up, and to such perfection has machinery attained, that the logs go in at one door, and come out at another fashioned in that remarkable style known here as "Eastlake," and which has become so much the fashion that grace and elegance are in danger of being taboo before long.

It was not to be long before the tide turned in Cook's direction. In the 1880s he, himself, could discern a change in fashion, a growing "taste for old things" well made:

This mania, as it is called by the scoffers, for old furniture is one of the best signs of returning good taste in a community that has long been the victim to the whims and impositions of foreign fashions.

The super-efficient factories of democratic America could just as easily turn away from European models and adopt those considered more native and "honest." In the 1890s and the early decades of the 20th century, furniture manufacturers began the production of bedroom sets in what was a "quaint" and no-less commercial style — that deemed "Colonial." In the hands of such craftsmen as Wallace Nutting, the furniture displayed some artistry, at least enough to cause confusion today when

Above: West bedroom, Thomas Ruggles House, Columbia Falls, Maine, 1818, built by Aaron Simmons Sherman. The four-poster with arched tester, the Empire country desk, and the Windsor chairs are harmonious and fitting period furnishings in this early-19th-century master bedroom.

Painted chairs, late 18th century. The use of paint and gilt to decorate furniture became very popular in the early 1800s. Sets of painted chairs were often used in the parlor and dining room, and some found their way to the bedrooms later in the century when the use of varnish and draping was preferred to painted decoration.

pieces are compared with the true antiques. The factories, however, issued forth carloads of maple and pine bedsteads, dressers, and chests which today have only the merit of being made of wood and not of composition board. It was no wonder that the work of such 1930s furniture designers as Russel Wright, Gilbert Rohde, and Donald Deskey has been recently acclaimed. Regardless of the merit of their designs, and these were considerable, it had been a long time since originality had been expressed in American furniture making.

Bedroom sets in various styles continue to this day to be popular. The number of pieces included in the usual ensemble, however, is only three or four. Not present are such standard Victorian objects as the washstand, dressing table or stand, bedside table or nightstand, and a whatnot or étagère. Also usually not included in the modern set is a wardrobe, the 19th-century's answer to the linen press. On occasion the Victorian bedroom also provided space for a sofa, reading table, and a secretary. The presence of so many different objects underlies the greater use of the bedroom at the time—as dressing room, a place to wash, and perhaps even as an area for the display of family treasures and mementoes.

During the late-Colonial period, the bedroom was similarly equipped to serve a number of familial and social functions. Although not as lavishly turned out as the mid-19th-century room, it was, nonetheless, a place where household accounts might be rendered, letters written, and even tea served to lady friends. Only during the early years of settlement when bedroom space was limited, and in recent years when a fmaily's evening and weekend activities have been moved to an enclosure termed

the "family room," have the bedchambers been devoid of the warmth and usefulness known throughout so much of American history. Now that homes are growing smaller because of prohibitive building and energy costs, there may be a rediscovery of the value of a well-designed bedroom area that affords not only a respite from daily life but a pleasant atmosphere for many satisfying household activities.

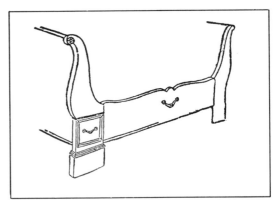

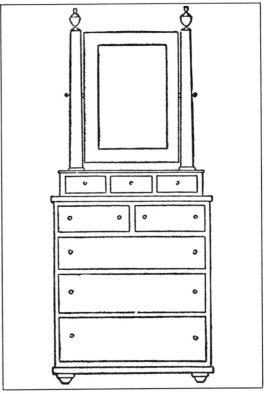

Victorian half-tester bed on posts, from A. J. Downing, *The Architecture of Country Houses* (1850).

Opposite page, (top): Sleigh bed, early 19th century. Also known as a "gondola" bed because of its outscrolled sides, this type of bedstead was one of the first of French inspiration to captivate the fashionable American public. *Opposite page (below):* Dresser with attached cheval mirror, early 19th century. This basic model was copied over and over again in the 20th century when so-called "Colonial" furniture styles were again popular. The finials on the posts are American Empire details which appear on many pieces of case furniture.

Above: Two designs for paneled beds with canopy and drapery, from Downing. In 1850 these were considered "modern" designs, that at left being in the "English taste" and the second "French."

Left: Iron bed from Montgomery Ward & Co.'s 1895 catalogue. Beds of this sort were rarely left in their original state, but were given an enamel "Japanning." The model illustrated was available in black, blue, maroon, and white. The top rods and knobs are of brass.

Mantel folding bed from Montgomery Ward & Co.'s 1895 catalogue. Not as famous as the Murphy model, the mantel bed nevertheless performed the same function of providing an uncluttered space by day and a restful abode by night. A hearth it was not.

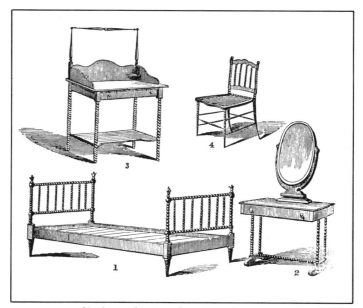

A cottage set of bedroom furniture from Downing was recommended for the simple dwelling. It was made of black walnut, maple, or birch and consisted of (1) bedstead, (2) dressing table with glass, (3) washstand with towel rack, and (4) a set of chairs. This could be purchased in 1850 for $36.

A cottage set of bedroom furniture from Downing consisting of (1) a dresser-bureau, (2) small table, (3) washstand, (4) a "French" or sleigh bed, and (5) four chairs. Downing does not provide details on the materials used, but, since this set costs only a dollar more than the one previously illustrated, it was most likely made of pine. The addition of marble tops would have increased the price.

Dressing table with hangings, from *Beautiful Homes* (1878) by Henry T. Williams and Mrs. C. S. Jones. What the ruffle hides from view is a slop pail and shelves that might contain other unsightly articles. This is a do-it-yourself project suggested by the authors, the base being formed from a pine box and the back cut out on the jig-saw, painted, and decorated in decalcomania.

Left: A French bureau was Clarence Cook's suggestion for a tasteful bedroom. In 1881 a piece such as this was more than likely to be found in a secondhand shop. In design it dates from the 1840s or '50s and may have been made of rosewood or walnut. Cook and other sophisticated patrons of fine furniture in the 1880s and '90s found such an object attractive because it was a useful piece that clearly proclaimed its purpose.

Below: Oak bedstead from Cook's *The House Beautiful*. The simple form of construction appealed to many devotees of straightforward bedroom furniture; metal beds were preferred for similar reasons.

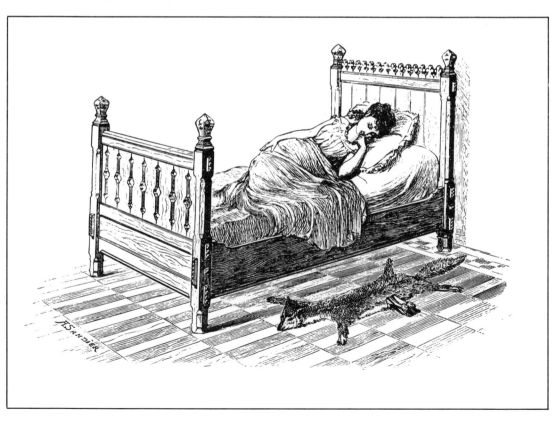

Opposite page (top): A washstand, dresser, and chamber suite from Montgomery Ward & Co.'s 1895 catalogue. All the pieces, except for the stand, are made of solid oak. The mirror on the dresser is of beveled glass. Once installed, the bed and dresser suite would probably not be moved for years; the combined weight was 300 pounds. Such solidity spelled "good taste" in homes from coast to coast in the late 19th and early 20th centuries.

Opposite page (below): Bedroom, James A. Allison Mansion, Indianapolis, Indiana, 1911-14, H. L. Bass, architect; the photograph dates from c. 1916. The caned bedroom set seen here reflects the Tudor Revival style preferred by America's upper class through the 1930s. The chairs and desk are probably copies of 17th-century designs.

This page (top): Block-front bureau, from Cook's *The House Beautiful.* In the East the passion for early American furniture increased each year from the 1880s, finally spreading during the 1920s and '30s to the whole country.

This page (below): The wing or easy chair, seen here in Hepplewhite's design book (1787), was welcomed back to many bedrooms during the rediscovery of 18th-century forms.

Illustration Credits

In this list of illustration credits, sources not specifically identified in the captions are given. The following abbreviations are used: a (above), b (below), m (middle), t (top), l (left), and r (right). Illustrations from the archives of the Historic American Buildings Survey (now part of the National Architectural and Engineering Record) housed at the Library of Congress are identified as LC-HABS. Those still housed at HABS are so designated. Illustrations from the Library of Congress collections are abbreviated as LC.

Cover/jacket: Mark Gottlieb (t,l); Michael Kanouff (b,l); Allison Abraham (t,r and b,r).

P.1, *The Cabinet-Maker and Upholsterer's Guide* (1794) by George Hepplewhite; p. 2, LC, Dorothea Lange; p.5, *The Architecture of Country Houses* (1850) by A. J. Downing; p. 7, *The Cabinet Maker's Assistant* (1853) by Blackie and Son.

Introduction: p. 9, LC-HABS, Cortlandt V. D. Hubbard (a), *Period Furnishings* (1914) by C. R. Clifford (l); p. 11, HABS (l), Clifford (l); p. 12, private collection.

1. *The Bedroom: A History:* p. 13, LC-HABS, Laurence E. Tilley (t and a); p. 15, LC, Dorothea Lange (t), LC, John Collier (m), *Early Connecticut Houses* (1900) by Norman M. Isham and Albert F. Brown (b); p. 16, Isham and Brown; p. 18, private collection (t and a); p. 19, LC-HABS (t), LC-HABS, Jack E. Boucher (m), LC-HABS, Laurence E. Tilley (b); p. 23, LC-HABS (t,r).

2. *The Essentials: Windows, Doors, Ceilings, and Floors:* p. 25, *Early Connecticut Houses* (1900) by Norman M. Isham

CALDWELL HOUSE

and Albert F. Brown (t), private collection (a); p. 26, HABS (t); p. 27, LC-HABS, Duane Garrett (b); p. 29, LC-HABS (t,l), Isham and Brown (t,r), *Early American Rooms, 1650-1858* (1936) by Russell Hawes Kettell (b); p. 31, LC-HABS (t and b).

3. *A Portfolio of Period Bedrooms:* pp. 33-36, Bert Denker; p. 37, Allison Abraham; pp. 38-50, Bert Denker; p. 51, Eugene Valenta; p. 52, Allison Abraham; pp. 53-54, Mark Gottlieb; p. 55, Allison Abraham; pp. 56-58, Mark Gottlieb; pp. 59-61, Michael Kanouff; pp. 62-64 (t), Allison Abraham; p. 64 (b), Michael Kanouff.

4. *The Architectural Furnishings: Millwork, Plasterwork, and Hardware:* p. 66, LC-HABS (r); p. 67, LC-HABS (m,l); p. 69, *Early Connecticut Houses* (1900) by Norman M. Isham and Albert F. Brown (t,l), LC-HABS, Jack E. Boucher (t,r).

5. *Paints, Papers, and Fabrics:* p. 71, LC-HABS, Cortlandt V. D. Hubbard; p. 73, LC-HABS (b); p. 76, *The Art Journal Illustrated Catalogue, The Industry of Nations 1851* (t,l), HABS (m); p. 77, HABS (t and b).

6. *Furnishing the Period Bedroom:* p. 79, HABS; p. 81, LC-HABS, Cortlandt V. D. Hubbard (t), *The Practical Book of Period Furniture* (1914) by Harold Donaldson Eberlein and Abbot McClure (b); p. 82, Eberlein and McClure (t and b); p. 88, HABS.

P. 90, *Early Connecticut Houses* (1900) by Norman M. Isham and Albert F. Brown; p. 91, Isham and Brown; p. 93, *Modern Architectural Designs and Details* (1881) by William T. Comstock; p. 95, Comstock.

JOHN BARNARD HOUSE HARTFORD

Selected Bibliography

Only those publications currently in print are included in this listing.

Benjamin, Asher. *The American Builder's Companion.* New York: Dover Publications, reprint 1969.

Bicknell, A. J. *Victorian Village Builder.* Watkins Glen, N.Y.: The American Life Foundation & Study Institute, reprint 1976.

Bicknell, A. J. and W. T. Comstock. *Victorian Architecture.* Watkins Glen, N.Y.: The American Life Foundation & Study Institute, reprint 1978.

Brightman, Anna. "Window Treatments for Historic Houses, 1700-1850." Technical Leaflet No. 17. Washington, D. C.: National Trust for Historic Preservation, n.d.

Cummings, Abbott Lowell. *Bed Hangings: A Treatise on Fabrics and Styles in the Curtaining of Beds, 1650-1850.* Boston: The Society for the Preservation of New England Antiquities, 1961.

_____. *Rural Household Inventories Establishing the Names, Uses, and Furnishings of Rooms in the Colonial New England Home.* Boston: The Society for the Preservation of New England Antiquities, 1964.

Downing, A. J. *The Architecture of Country Houses.* New York: Dover Publications, reprint 1969.

Eastlake, Charles Locke. *Hints on Household Taste.* New York: Dover Publications, reprint 1969.

Frangiamore, Catherine Lynn. *Wallpapers in Historic Preservation.* National Park Service Publication No. 185, Technical Preservation Services Division. Washington, D.C.: Office of Archeology and Historic Preservation, 1977.

Handlin, David P. *The American Home, Architecture and Society, 1815-1915.* Boston: Little, Brown and Co., 1979.

Little, Nina Fletcher. "Historic Houses: An Approach to Furnishing." Technical Leaflet No. 17. Nashville, Tenn.: American Association for State and Local History, 1970.

Loth, Calder and Julius Trousdale Sadler, Jr. *The Only Proper Style, Gothic Architecture in America.* Boston: New York Graphic Society, 1975.

Nylander, Jane C. *Fabrics for Historic Buildings.* Washington, D.C.: The Preservation Press, 1977.

Page, Marian. *Historic Houses Restored and Preserved.* New York: Whitney Library of Design, 1976.

Peterson, Harold L. *American Interiors from Colonial Times to the Late Victorians.* New York: Charles Scribner's Sons, 1971.

Seale, William. *Recreating the Historic House Interior.* Nashville, Tenn.: American Association for State and Local History, 1979.

_____. *The Tasteful Interlude: American Interiors through the Camera's Eye.* New York: Dover Publications, 1975.

Vaux, Calvert. *Villas and Cottages.* New York: Dover Publications, reprint 1970.

Wharton, Edith and Ogden Codman, Jr. *The Decoration of Houses.* New York: W. W. Norton & Co., reprint 1978.

Whiffen, Marcus. *American Architecture Since 1780.* Cambridge, Mass.: The M.I.T. Press, 1969.

Index

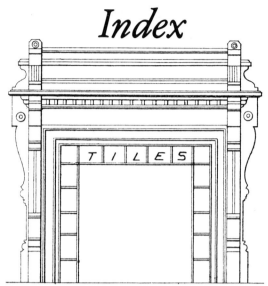

TILES

DORUS BARNARD HOUSE
HARTFORD.

People who live in and love old houses (or new houses in a traditional style) are constantly searching for ideas, products, and services to improve their homes.

In our effort to bring you the best possible information on old houses, we hope you will share your expertise with us. We would like to know what products or services you would recommend that we might consider for inclusion in the next edition of THE BRAND NEW OLD HOUSE CATALOGUE. And we hope you will let us know what titles would be helpful additions to our OLD HOUSE series.

Please send your recommendations to: Lawrence Grow, c/o Special Sales Department, Warner Books, 75 Rockefeller Plaza, New York, N.Y. 10019.

THE OLD HOUSE BOOKS

Edited by Lawrence Grow

THE BRAND NEW OLD HOUSE CATALOGUE

3,000 Completely New and Useful Products, Services, and Suppliers for Restoring, Decorating, and Furnishing the Period House—From Early American to 1930s Modern

#97-557 224 pages $9.95 in quality paperback; $17.95 in hardcover

THE OLD HOUSE BOOK OF BEDROOMS

96 pages, including 32 color pages

#97-553 $7.95 in quality paperback; $15.00 in hardcover

THE OLD HOUSE BOOK OF LIVING ROOMS AND PARLORS

96 pages, including 32 color pages

#97-552 $7.95 in quality paperback; $15.00 in hardcover

Forthcoming:

THE OLD HOUSE BOOK OF OUTDOOR LIVING SPACES
THE OLD HOUSE BOOK OF DINING ROOMS AND KITCHENS
THE OLD HOUSE BOOK OF HALLS AND STAIRCASES

Look for these books in your favorite bookstore. If you can't find them, you may order directly by sending your check or money order for the retail price of the book plus 50¢ per order and 50¢ per book to cover postage and handling to: Warner Books, P.O. Box 690, New York, N.Y. 10019. N.Y. State and California residents, please add sales tax.